From the Mists of Time

From the Mists of Time

Poetry & Prose

✷ ✷ ✷

Trudy Myrrh Reagan

2024

Copyright © 2024
MYRRH
All Rights Reserved.

✸ ✸ ✸

ISBN: 978-1-7342742-7-1

myrrh-art.com
trudy@myrrh-art.com

Cover Image: Westtown School. Watercolor by Myrrh, 1953.

To Philip, the scientist, and Helen, the poet—
my parents who took me for walks and read to me.

CONTENTS

✷ ✷ ✷

POETRY & PROSE

    1   TO OUR CONNECTONE

I. I WAS BORN

    5   MY MOTHER, 1908-2006
    6   AS TIME LENGTHENS
    7   HELEN EXPECTANT
    8   THIS CAME FIRST
    9   TO IOWA CITY 1938

II. ELKTON, VA 1939-1940

    13   COLOR CRAYONS
    14   ELKTON, VA
    15   THE BLUE RIDGE MOUNTAINS
    16   NEW PENNY
    17   SUMMERY DAY

III. ARLINGTON, VA 1941-1947

    21   COLOR WHEEL
    22   IN THE WOODS I
    23   IN THE WOODS II
    24   BURROWING
    26   WHITE

III. ARLINGTON, VA 1941-1947 [CONT'D.]

26	VICTORIANS
27	VERGE
28	CABIN JOHN CAR
29	WINTER
30	ONLY AT NIGHT
32	WITCH HAZEL
34	THE BAY WINDOW
36	PARTIES
37	AIRBORNE

IV. GATLINGBURG, TN 1947-1951

41	MOVING TO GATLINGBURG
45	GLINT
46	1946
47	1947
48	1949
49	1950
50	WALKING TO A SMOKY MOUNTAIN SCHOOL
53	SMOKE
54	WILD PLUM PICKING
55	MRS. SIMMS
56	BIBLE LESSONS
57	BIBLE SCHOOL
58	EASTER
59	ODE TO SENATOR TALMADGE
60	HEADING NORTH
61	SPELUNKERS

III. GATLINBURG, TN 1947-1951 [CONT'D.]

- 62 BALDS AND COVES
- 65 SCOURED EARTH
- 66 DRIVING THERE
- 67 ROOSTER
- 68 TRUDGING

IV. WESTTOWN FRIENDS SCHOOL 1951-1954

- 73 WHEN I WAS YOUNG
- 74 PREMONITION
- 75 AUTOMAT OF THE INTELLECT
- 76 HOAGIES
- 78 WONDER DRUG
- 79 VISIT HOME
- 80 HARKENING BACK
- 82 DIMENSIONS

- 84 LIST OF ILLUSTRATIONS
- 87 ACKNOWLEDGEMENTS
- 88 COLOPHON

Poetry & Prose

TO OUR CONNECTOME

To our connectone, so much more
than a bundle of neurons in our head
it already formed synapes, reacting in the womb
to joys, talents, and stresses of the other, the mother
together with little inherited formations.

In babyhood each stimulus registers
helps form a mesh of paths uniquely ours
pathways of common sense about space and time
our language sensibilities, each of us in our own way.

And throughout life augmenting or surmounting
our inherited personality traits forming
elaborating, or muffling constellations
of recognition, communities of relationships
litanies of responses:
an encyclopedia of connections
possibilities uniquely ours.

Where is the soul? Is it real?
My dear husband's connectome answers: Yes!

Four days after he died, I hurt my hand
in a freak accident. My ring finger began
to swell and turn blue. They had to cut off
my wedding ring.

I.

I WAS BORN…
my parents were
Philip King, 1903-1974
Helen Carter King, 1908-2006

The act of anticipation no longer
tantalized, but simply hovered
like the tail of a comet imitating
the plunge of a shooting star
night after night.

In her bed of reason, she watched
decades go by, haunted with
dreams of open sky.

So like my mother...

MY MOTHER, 1908-2006

She looked back on how she'd picked her mate,
much like the choice of name for her first child:
A compromise, predictable and mild,
avoiding qualities she might come to hate.

She had prowled the garrets, the best soirées in town
for every frenetic bash and soul untamed,
accumulating nights of ecstasy and pain.
She hungered for a way to settle down.

At last the hour had come to play it safe.
The years ahead would need a different guise.
Without flinching, she accepted this with open eyes:
Convention was a jacket that would chafe.

In her bed of reason, she watched decades go by,
haunted with dreams of open sky.

AS TIME LENGTHENS

While her young geologist husband
carefully picked his way across, up the ledges
of Guadalupe Peak in Texas, filling his heavy pack
with fossils from an ancient reef,
Helen, before she was my mother, whiled away
her time in a two-room cabin on the desert floor.

To kill time, she planned a crocheted tablecloth
that would grace their return to civilization.
No radio helped her pass the time in 1934,
as the foot-wide runner grew to fifteen feet,
and marked a prodigious number of hours.

At 90, Helen took up crocheting again,
this time with coarser yarn. Playful hats
that matched my coats, and those that didn't,
grew from her fingertips. Those that we still keep
lie in a bedroom drawer, a witness,
along with the fine ecru fifteen-foot roll,
which might unravel if I cut it,
Time Incarnate.

In her last hour, I counted the seconds
between breaths. Each came more slowly
than the last. When no more came,
I still kept hold of her hand. Somewhere
inside her thumb, a small pulse ticked.

At the mortuary, as always happens,
Helen's fingernails grew.

HELEN EXPECTANT

Helen's bare belly bulged
so long past the due date
that the breathless counting
toward the arrival was blunted,
then forgotten.
She baked and sewed,
suspended in tranquility.
while her dear Philip-O
read her *War and Peace,*
in a pleasurable drone.

The act of anticipation no longer
tantalized, but simply hovered
like the tail of a comet imitating
the plunge of a shooting star
night after night.

Grandmother Alma, too,
was past counting backwards
from that indefinite due date
of her demise.
She simply lived, listing rightward
in her chair like an old beached boat
braced in the sand against a storm.

Yet, time did move. Helen delivered
a nine-pound grandchild, then Alma died.

THIS CAME FIRST: Muttering to each other, soft other mothers and mothers speaking like radios left running like water, motors and brothers running and running...What else could I do, slumping into people's arms, but relieve myself, giving myself over...and over to the pearly, endless rumble of the ocean, escaping beyond wishing, since wishing anyway was way beyond my thinking of it?

TO IOWA CITY 1938

Going and Going...

Electric wires go up and down.
My toys, my toys we left behind!
The moon came with us, but now he's gone.

Electric wires go up and down.
Trees in the fields, they lose the race
with fences and trees and rocks and signs.

Electric wires go up and down.
Way yonder, wee trees slide by real slow.
A house, a store, a funny car
electric wires go up and down.

I have a friend way at the edge
in red and white on tall, tall legs:
My water tank. He *almost* stays...

And as he goes, here comes his friend,
he's green, out at the edge, out at the edge.
Two, Mama, two!

II.

ELKTON, VA 1939-1940...
In the Blue Ridge Mountains

It was the beginning of awareness ...
At four, my memories were disjointed jewels.

COLOR CRAYONS

When I was four,
the neighbor girls took me
to school like Mary's lamb
upstairs in the dusty wooden building
in the nice room with blue paint
and breezy open windows
and a nice empty view of sky...

And seats where two could sit
except I wiggled, so the teacher
just had to move me into the corner
and sit me down on the floor with crayons.

And I colored a nice map
of the Blue Ridge Mountains
the Green Ridge
the Red Ridge
and the Yellow Ridge...

ELKTON, VA
about my father

My father was hired by the U.S. Geological Survey in 1930 as part of a large contingent of explorers whose job it was to complete the geological mapping of the entire country. I was three when we moved to Elkton, Virginia in the Blue Ridge Mountains.

In those days, it was very small, surrounded by pastures and farmland. Virginia is blessed wih parallel Applachian ridges and flat, picturesque valleys in between them. The modest Shennadoah River coursed a few blocks away from our home in town.

It was the beginning of awareness and memory for me. Every noon I would race to the fence corner of the Spotswood Lodging house and tavern to watch the mail train arrive, a few blocks away, chugging smoke. The room beside ours became vacant, with an even better view. Once, I rushed into that room and interrupted a couple kissing.

My memories are disjointed jewels...

THE BLUE RIDGE MOUNTAINS

The sky and morning-glory blue ridges
lay one behind the other in the hazy sun.

Every morning
I let them speak to me, tell me, ask me
My One Great Wish: *Come over here
and play In our big blue backyard!*

NEW PENNY

Nothing cleans the air
like the year's
first robust
bird song

Here I am
three years old again
bright as a new penny

freed from notices
that come in the mail
all that botheration

SUMMERY DAY

Our little walk along open meadows ended at a shady line of trees along the river—the Shenandoah.

We could see patches of sky between the maple leaves when the wind blew. The road ended at the water's edge. My mother sat down on the concrete, with Emily and me on either side in the shade.

We threw pebbles in the water. We were both four.

Trees met overhead	ferns and moss covered the banks
wind rustled the leaves	water ripples slid over stones.
We sat on concrete	dangling our legs.
Across the river	we saw more concrete
and the road.	Mother said it was for the other side
of a bridge	no longer there.
I worried	about cars falling in.

III.

ARLINGTON, VA 1941-1945...
During World War Two, with vists to relatives in Georgetown, DC

*Two great gifts my parents gave me:
Father read to me, and Mother took me
on her early morning walks.*

COLOR WHEEL

Red was for cherry cough syrup and the clove taste
of Lavoris.

Orange was for mercurachrome, thin and iridescent
painted on cuts with a glass rod.

Yellow was for cod liver oil, fat Sulfa pills, Butisin Picrate
burn ointment, mustard plaster applied hot to the chest
for congestion.

Green was for tincture of green soap, also iridescent
and disinfecting.

Blue was for the deep blue glass bottle of Milk of Magnesia.

Violet was for Genetian Violet, for impetigo sores.

White was for cold cream, zinc ointment for scabs and
sunburned noses, and band-aids that kept coming off.

Brown was for iodine, Sal Hepatica laxative, and
for too-old Argerol stinging in my nose.

IN THE WOODS I

Trees
in fading light.
Mother and small girl, hands held,
move as one
without words
both beg:
Not yet. Go slow, Wait.
Each lingers
for the other's sake, feeling
woods-at-dusk
with no spoken way to tell
the other what moves her so.

IN THE WOODS II

Far off, two figures move in the late afternoon shade, a mother and small girl. Why does this sight touch me so? Do I put myself in the shoes of the mother or the child? Neither and both. I have been both.

Each knows the other often darts off before she is ready, expects it, knows that when this happens she must follow. But she wants to stay: She feels a little anxious. Yet each notices that the other is subdued by the almost-evening light, the high, over-arching trees. A sense of the other partner, a bond not to break the mood forms, and restless impulses are brushed away.

Neither says much about where they find themselves.

What would be the use? One partner has too few words to tell it, the other too many, too nuanced.

Each only knows what she herself is feeling. Having felt both, I witness the harmony in this counterpoint.

BURROWING

Peekaboo becomes hiding, Hide-and-seek, and forts.
Ours weren't in trees.

In 1944, we knew that safety was in holes: fox holes.

Men did it. Men crouched in the belly of bomber planes.
Lenny and I struggled on our bellies, covered by a wooden
crate and went *ackity-ack-ack* at the enemy.

In the midst of this vivid thrill I suddenly watched myself
doing it, and wondered about the land of make-believe.

Later, there were the trenches in his back yard, six of us
energetically digging, finding neat things and tunneling,
tunneling, imagining coming out on the other side the fence
till the worried mother came out one night and smashed it in
lest it collapse on us

Later, in a web of trenches dug for a new sewer, we could go
down briefly six feet into the layers of yellow-brown clay and
find the forgotten realm again.

WHITE

When I was little, Pasteur's theory of infectious germs
was only decades old.

You remember how the nurses all wore white? SANITARY,
so reassuring, with their starchy, germ-free caps. They were
white-crowned goddesses to be obeyed.

Our new, all-white suburban bathroom, was cleaner than
anything in homes before, more SANITARY. On the white
porcelain floor tiles, take care!

The slippery glass shampoo bottle might break,
Breck shampoo, or Halo:
"Hal-O, everybody, Hal-O, Halo is the shampoo
that glorifies your hair..."
Singing commercials were new.

Now, I was able to bathe by myself, (sanitary!), glorifying my
stupid straight hair with soapy suds, piling it up in loopy curls.

My hair was as beauty-queen white as the platinum blonde
on the silver screen preening in black and white before a great
round mirror.

I leaned on the white basin, peered into the mirror of the
medicine cabinet, giggling at my lathery glamour.

VICTORIANS

How long ago it seems
when windows were built like eyes
with brows above.

The simple arches showed approval
the wrinkled ones frowned: *Not So Good.*

Like Aunt Gertrude's creases above
her pince-nez spectacles.

All that pince-ing made her tense
between the eyes (to say nothing of the
exquisite pain of all her Antebellum etiquette).

VERGE

We learn a lot, you and I, about the world
on the verge of sleep.

The deep-throated rumble of cities
the flicker of shadows in a zombie to-and-fro
from the street.

In the kitchen
the savage clink of spoons on cups
and a stream of various voices
spilling over the dishes
another flowing through
sluice-gates off and on
through the telephone.

CABIN JOHN CAR

M Street, Georgetown, Washington, DC, 1942

Cars rattled along on cobblestones. But the trolley cars were new, streamlined, gliding on newly-laid rails. With wheels concealed like the feet of women in hoop skirts, they moved with dignity, almost floating. Concealed, too, was their power source, underground, until you rode to the outskirts, where the conductor hopped out to put a trolley up to reach the overhead wire. These were the sleek and rounded St. Louis Car Co. streetcars, which replaced the angular all-wood models that resembled Victorian houses.

To reach Glen Echo Amusement Park, our car glided along the Potomac and the C & O Canal heading upstream, sometimes on trestles, sometimes on embankments where honeysuckle vines brushed against the windows.

Through the dense foliage, I caught glimpses of white frame houses, as sturdy and authoritative as an old lady's Cuban heel Oxford shoe. Riverside houses with screened windows, screened doors, long screened porches poised against bugs.

But mostly these were hidden behind monumental leafed-out oaks and maples. The cumulus wall of green contrasted with grey—the grey of screens, of drab sky, of driveways spread with sharp coal clinkers from the furnace.

On weekends, the cars were full. Glen Echo was a mish-mosh of carnival games, wild rides, and band music echoing across acres of families picnicing. A shady field was full of white wooden glider swings, where we could sit across from each other, chatting and pushing ourselves to and fro. Striped canvas canopies on them protected us from scattered showers, stiff little awnings in dark green, orange and yellow, hideous colors, with thin stripes of black.

WINTER

The street and sky emanate power for ill: Menace
the dread of more snow felt in the nostrils.

Thinking of my sled,

I wince with pleasure, remembering
numbly pulling the sled uphill,
in the deep blue-grey dusk

Remembering
my perverse satisfaction
of enduring another and another
turn before dark.

ONLY AT NIGHT

I only knew what they looked like at night, the places on the way to Uncle Charlie's, for we only went there for evening parties. The part I never saw by day came after Key Bridge, after the brick colonial buildings where Ger and Harry lived in Georgetown, and past majestic downtown Washington where everything looked famous.

I had a desperate urge always to know where I was, so I gradually learned the changes in neighborhood by styles in architecture. First, brick apartments sprinkled with colonial cupolas like a hundred Mount Vernons, then heavy-set townhouses with trees near the zoo, and finally the long prospect of new, slab-sided apartment buildings, and streetlights marching uphill and down, like drapes of chains turned upside-down. Charlie's neighborhood was one where no trees grew.

Daddy was really taken with my neighborhood I.D. game when I finally happened to mention it near the zoo one night. "Just proves what I've said, Daddy's girl has a Bump of Locality."

The last Christmas Eve we were in the Washington area was when we had sleet, and Daddy decided to go on to Charlie's Christmas party anyway. I was in fifth grade, and by now it was really getting tight for the three of us in the front seat of our '39 Ford. Daddy could hardly move the gearstick between us on the floor.

We hadn't even gotten as far as Key Bridge when Whack! a heavy ol' ice ball made shatter marks spread across the windshield on Mama's side. With the car slipping around like me in galoshes on ice, I was too scared to play the game. The nearly-empty streets spooked me.

Poor Charlie! Hardly anyone was there. I sat on the studio couch and stared at the granny-square afghan that Aunt Kitty had made, then saw how the two framed still-lifes really stood out on the grey walls. These were pastels of bean pots and glass bottles Daddy and Mama had given him. Daddy had drawn them himself ages ago in college.

Charlie wasn't married, so he stood around waiting for his sister Ger to come and play carols and sister Kitty to bring eats. Not tonight. And without my Aunt Dot and ol' Albert, there wouldn't be many jokes. Charlie carried on his familiar refrain about how he would buy himself a house, and an electric organ. Then we could really sing!

Finally, Daddy said awkwardly, "Well, we have to be getting back. It'll take extra long to get home tonight," not mentioning the windshield.

On Christmas Day I got everything I wanted for a change: Three Nancy Drew mysteries, an oil paint set, and a pair of bunny fur slippers, but I caught a messy cold.

WITCH HAZEL

My real grandmother had died young, but Aunt Ger, her older sister, made a good substitute. Aunt Ger's house had odd smells—Witch Hazel, for starters. It was weirder and wilder-smelling than rubbing alcohol. The overall and lasting smell in the room was a liniment with a clean, spicy smell I learned years later was tea tree oil. On her bureau I lifted the lids of nail polish lacquer, colognes, but my favorite was Pacquins cold cream. I liked it the same way I liked the smell of baby powder.

Her implements were odd, too: metal clamps for Marcelling her hair, a chamois buffing tool for shining her nails, hair nets, a worn pumice stone.

Downstairs, the closet under the stairs smelled of the cedar chest and the cedar coat rack my mother had chip-carved in fifth grade. Uncle Harry kept his guitar there.

I could count on Aunt Ger to keep the furniture the same: The far end of the room was dominated by a monumental scroll-sided bookcase. Above it was a bas-relief of George Washington ("Where did that get to?" my mother asks "so valuable...it was done when Washington was still alive."). There were also watercolors of an early American flag and a Confederate one by the same artist. The shelves were full of sets of leather-bound books of classics that no one read.

At the other end near the front door was a massive table with marble top that matched this in style, and a mirror over it. A narrow shelf underneath held a tall Chinese vase with a round lid. When I was the only child at parties, I crouched and sat on the shelf, then lifted the lid, fingering the dried rose petals and coming back again and again to take in the dark, spicy fragrance.

In the middle of the room, on the mantle, was a wonderful chiming Scottish clock which Uncle Harry made a ritual of winding with a fist-sized key before he and Ger sat down for their noontime beer and barley soup. Once, I demanded a taste of Budweiser. One was enough! It was awful. They laughed.

Also in the middle of the room were high-backed occasional chairs with claw feet just like the bathtub, and a sofa, where Harry, ever restless, would sit, swinging his foot, waiting for anyone to be garrulous with. Taciturne Ger was not much company. She had developed selective deafness in her later years. It was her excuse to turn up the radio, or after 1947, the TV.

Once in a long while, I would follow Harry down the steep steps —almost a ladder—into the poorly-lit and musty basement, where he carved off the thinnest imaginable slices of ham for sandwiches from the man-sized Smithfield ham strung up, all chalky with mold on the outside. This made ham sandwiches that were zingy, like bacon, only better, and very salty. And several meals later, hash, ground with a hand grinder.

In the basement corner was a peeling leather steamer trunk full the to brim with mildewing Confederate money. He said no, you couldn't spend it, so I was really puzzled. What was it doing there?

(Helens comments: Their wedding outfits were in there, too. I told the movers, Leave that one! so of course, they took it.)

THE BAY WINDOW

The desk by the bay window had a drawer for me with a big book. It had no writing and no lines. Gradually I filled it with drawings of houses and clouds, girls with silly shoes, B-29s and fellows saying "Huh??!!"

The sun came through the window in the morning while I played shellac records with a reed needle: *Dear Little Cookie Bush, down where the green grass grows . . . Snoop Wiggie, snoop wiggie . . .*

The upright piano stood here, too. Sometimes Aunt Ger would just sit down at it with no one asking her to do it and spin out long pieces by Schubert and Schumann (a distant relative). I was supposed to practice and didn't.

This nook was separated from the fireplace in their long room by a sofa with lion claw feet that jutted out. Harry would stretch out on it after a long walk along the C & O Canal with me, and I would land on him, merciless: "Tickle me!"

"Lauda mercy chile, you gotta let yo ol' Uncle Harry rest, I got I got the epizooatic."

Sometimes he blurted out, "Great dan a-mawnin' . . . jes look at 'em go!" I thought this was *Great Dane a morning . . .* which didn't make much sense, but neither did "I knowd ya when y' wuh knee-high to a grasshoppa!"

It took me 40 years to learn that epizootic was a real word. They had no toys for me there, so they let me rummage in the drawer full of knickknacks: golf tees, bridge apparatus and poker chips, old gun shells. When you flipped the curlique bridge thing, it sometimes said Trump. They let me hold the scrimshaw whale tooth and look at the little Esquimos engraved on it, and play tea set with the Chinese cloissine. After 1949, Ger remarked, "You just can't get that anymore!"

In the kitchen, the floor sloped. I found this out with my marble. Before I learned geography in school, I saw the oil cloth map above the kitchen table. "That's Europe," Ger told me. She pointed out the countries: Greece? and Hungary?? and Turkey??? HAH HAH HAH.

PARTIES

On the floor there was a curious kilim rug. I first noticed it at my fourth birthday party. It had deep red angular, twisted keys on a blue green background, but rows in different sizes, uneven. This was something I could focus on as the grown-ups talked, for I had no cousins. I also liked the big birthday card with the yellow 4 on it.

The life of the party were Aunt Dot and Uncle Albert Denim. He looked like a card shark with gold teeth. They were grafted onto the family, because Tom, the relative who had married Dot, had died in the great flu epidemic after World War One, leaving her with two little daughters, Joanne and Louise. She'd remarried. Albert was as slim as Dot was hefty. He wisecracked and her big chest vibrated with unladylike guffaws.

When they all crowded around the upright piano to sing, I got good at hearing a note, anticipating the next and chiming in. My dad, on the other hand, could never match any note, but he bellowed with gusto. Mama and her very musical Whittlesey aunts and uncles carried the day, and carols with them made Christmas complete.

Later, when they sent me to bed, I could quietly sit on the top step and peer through the bannisters. The hum of conversation and laughter below was monotonous, but the anticipation of getting caught kept me sitting on little pins.

AIRBORNE
Rock Creek Park, Washington DC, 1944

Airborne,
always a miracle,
even on playground swings
having very, very long chains.

Backing up, up on tiptoe,
The seat tight against my small butt
I kick up!

For takeoff
over the steep slope below
down to Rock Creek

Slope covered with oak leaves
brown... withered

I go free,
into the sky of bare branches
over the trunks and twigs.

Flecks of white between them
giving hints of distant walls
across the gorge.

Untethered, free
until the inevitable Return

IV.

GATLINBURG, TN 1947-1951...

Population 1,400, Gateway to the
Great Smoky Mountains National Park
only 13 years old at the time.

Come along I sense
—a treasure
This particularly
clear, crisp air of autumn
tinged with wisps of smoke

takes me back to the first
woodstove fire of yore
the pot-bellied stove

a treasure, being twelve again
running to school

MOVING TO GATLINBURG

"There I sat on Buttermilk Hill, watching all the soldiers drill," I sang on my hill looking down on the tidy brick houses of my neighborhood, seven miles from the Washington Monument. Me, not yet ten years old, sensed this was the last look, I savored it. It was now winter and my father had just received his USGS assignment: To map geographically the Great Smoky Mountains in Tennessee. I tried to imagine Tennessee with country roads, everything covered in green moss. I said goodbye to bus rides to school.

I was an only child. This was a good thing, because our 1939 Ford convertible had only one seat across the front, and I was already too big to be comfortable sharing it with my parents and the stick gearshift. It was a two-day drive to Gatlinburg, Tennessee.

After Knoxville, we passed miles of winter pastures with weeds and golden hay stubble ringed by rail fences, off in the distance, hazy blue ridges.

From the open pastures of Pigeon Forge, the road took aim at the mountains. The highway was a narrow two-lane one, rough to drive. It began to wind, curve after curve, along the a river with rapids. Occasionally, some barns displayed wall-size black-and-white letters announcing "See Seven States from Lookout Mountain" or "Triple-treated Garrett Snuff," otherwise they were left unpainted. Untidy barns and cabin homes in shades of warm gray: nothing new except for tin roofs. In sloping front yards, cars were up on blocks. And *washing machines* on front porches, so surprising!

Finally, the road opened out to a town with a four-lane concrete main street two miles long, built by the WPA in the 1930s. The street was lined with six large stone hotels—the tourist desination, Gateway to the Smokies.

Our temporary home on Roaring Fork Road was a unit in a tourist court. We now call these motels. Our sweet landlady chewed stuff. The inside of her mouth was brown with it. Assigned to show me to school was little Henrietta Reagan in blue jeans, cuffs rolled up a hitch. It turned out that everyone wore these, both boys and girls. I was used to little pastel dresses with embroidery.

My route to school was a mile over hill and dale. I would discover her house had a hand pump, an outdoor privy, a radio, and one of those washing machines on the porch.

In my fifth grade class, they thought I talked funny. the teacher thought I was disrespectful, but I couldn't understand what she was telling me. I wasn't good at sports, not even horseshoes. We had forty students in the room, old desks that had holes for inkwells. Some kids had socks too small, ones that slid into their shoe; or the back of their shoes were pounded down to accommodate their growing feet. This state did not provide us with books. We had old textbooks, tattered and marked up. The next year in 1948 the geography books all changed. We had to buy new ones. We really noticed new names of old colonies. When the furnace went out, we were kept in for an hour to see if the heat of 40 bodies helped, and if not, we were sent home.

In the winter, there was always the aroma of smoke in the air. This spelled warmth, the sum of mountain cabins heated with potbelly stoves. I walked to school down the Main Street, where

in the distance snowy white Mount LeConte at over 6,500 feet had surprising blue shadows. This walk was on the main drag, but sometimes I chose the old, rutted River Road behind some of the hotels to enjoy the water rapids and its gristmill in disrepair. I would linger on the wooden bridge at the river's narrow point. The surface was untroubled, the water a deep green. I thought about "still waters run deep."

One morning I paused at a whole garden of lacy asparagus ferns, each little needle with its own coating of glistening frost.

My walk home was full of music, my music, music of songs we had just sung with Miss Armstrong at school.

With these walks, I began to feel at home. This feeling deepened when the mystery of the outdoor washing machines was revealed to me: rural electrification came late here, made possible by the building of dams through the funding of the TVA, the Tennessee Valley Authority, voted on during FDR's administration.

Electricity meant washing machines, every woman's ardent wish at the time. However, if her house was built before 1940, she had to place the washing machine on the porch. There was no room inside for one.

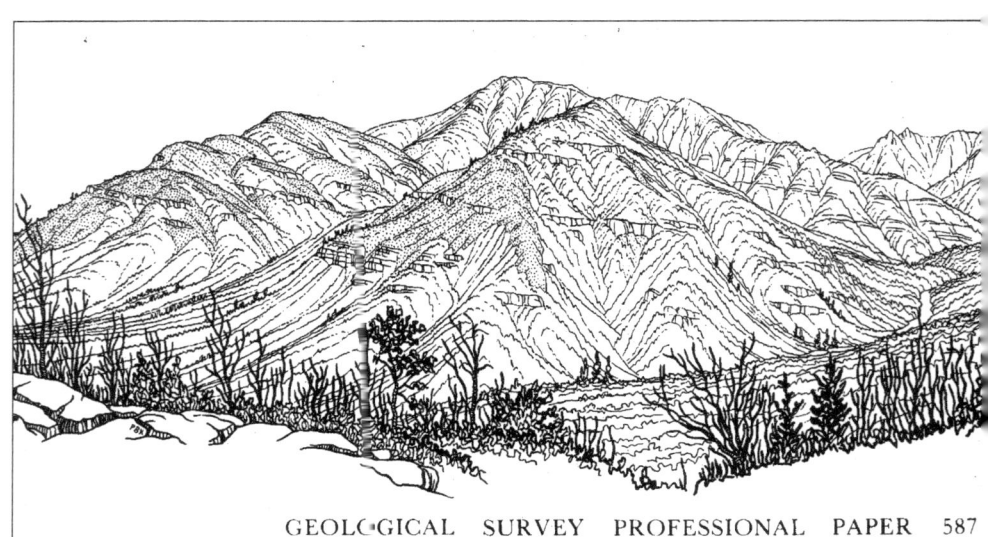

GEOLOGICAL SURVEY PROFESSIONAL PAPER 587

GLINT

In a valley of carpenters
early autumn mornings
with the golden smell
of sawed wood

Today,
anticipation
of the disk-saws whining
and the ring
of the arhythmic hammer
falling
on the drums
of joisted house frames

Echoing between the ridges
of mountains
making their silence sing

1946

When I was old enough to wonder about stuff
Zippers were as mysterious to me as
Kleenex popping up out of a box.

My father hated radio, didn't want it.
Great Aunt Gertrude was getting an FM.
She gave away her AM radio for my room.

My secret was
learning the best stations
the farthest away, from across oceans
came in clearly on short wave in the dead of night
while I gazed dreamily at the back of the set
at its little glowing amber city of skyscrapers that made it go.
Until
Mother found out it kept me up late.

1947

Through pitch-dark fields toward me
closer and closer
come misaligned yellow headlights
bobbing and dipping on the rutted road
like a couple of puppies
sniffing their way home.

The pickup comes into view,
to the store lit by a lone neon sign
that reads EAT.

The nose of the track as long as a hound's,
fenders and shiny bumpers
curved in an eager grin,
the bugged-out headlight eyes close together.
It turns, spinning around noisily
in the gravel, goes scuffling off into the night
with red tail lights dimmed by dust.

Overhead, a rare night-flying DC-3
propeller plane rumbles and bumbles
taking so long to labor
from left to right across the speckled sky
that I'm distracted by owls and fireflies
the other occasional pairs of the lights flashing.

1949

My mother threw out the paperback
The Well of Loneliness
before I had a chance to read it.
She hissed: "It's about lesbians"
and let it go at that.

After menarche
she showed me about Kotex.
She said in the old days
they used cotton rags.
She lost her mother at age six,
so, when she saw blood on the rags,
she thought her dear Aunt Ger
must really be sick.
She laughed at the memory.

Me, struggling
in a beat-up school bathroom stall
with a box I bought with my own money.
I studied the directions again
and felt around Down There
unable to find the hole
to put the Tampax in.

1950

After the realism of
the Depression and World War Two
we inhabited a dream house
of unyielding newness.
Both parents gloated, my father
forever painting away imperfections
with the just-invented latex paint
my mother, like models on TV, like our new TV!
daily polishing the kitchen with miracle products
to mend the broken snow.

WALKING TO A SMOKY MOUNTAIN SCHOOL

I was lucky enough to have a long walk to school.

I had to walk in the autumn, smelling again the smoke of wood stoves after a long, muggy summer. Little curls of smoke dotted the hillsides. I shuffled through corridors of scarlet maple leaves, overhead and knee deep.

In winter, I had to walk before the sun was up, and watch the creeping transformation from dark grey to green in hemlock boughs. It was frosty. I had ear-muffs on. The path led through a farm, past feathery asparagus fronds dusted lightly with pretend powdered sugar.

I had to walk in fresh snow, blazing new trails with my galoshes at the base of mounded-up-ice-cream Mt. Leconte in blue shadows.

I had to walk in the rain, and in my primitive mind, wet colors had tastes: Some oily and dark like greasy gravy or dark green enamel paint, some light and chalky like Pepto-Bismol. The combination fascinated me. The Judas tree at the stile wept red-violet buds through its bark. To amuse myself, I sang.

SMOKE

Years before smog alerts and no-burn days
even before they paved our street
every autumn day brought smoke.

We waded in leaves from
scarlet maples, copper beeches,
walnut and cottonwood.
They had to be disposed of.

With bamboo rakes we would fill
wooden bushel baskets with them,
dumping them by the rocks
that served as a curb, piling them up
even as the Entropy Kids wallowed
and burrowed and belly-flopped in them.
Exasperated,
we regathered this scattering
into a tight pile and set it alight

Redoubling our efforts,
we tackled the other side of the yard.
Now, like greyed-out paper dolls
in dirndl skirts, we raked and
bent and bobbed about.

As the October sun descended,
our silhouettes merged
into various phantoms, casting shafts
of shadows into the billowing incense.

WILD PLUM PICKING

It takes energy to keep up with the rank vegetation hereabouts. Over there is a field they forgot, with second-growth beginning, sprouts of briars. Somewhere nearby are the old gravestones we found once, not very legible anymore, since someone chose the local shale to carve on. A child can carve it.

A little dusty from the dirt road here, and hot, I'm standing in the thicket of high plum bushes and other weeds, some with thorns, some smelling of hay. These bushes seem permanent: could it be, this patch was never cut over? My mother is out of sight, filling her bucket, watching out for copperheads as well as rattlers. (We had water moccasins, too. Do they just live in the water? They never told me.) I don't bother to taste what I'm picking. I know it's tart.

Locusts wheeze, the afternoon shadows grow heavy. The mourning doves round jug-whistle call repeats and repeats. Plaintive flatted notes in a cozy Tennessee thicket. Through my blanket of solitude comes the thin sound of hillbilly radio music from the only house downhill: raucous but sweetly predictable. From this distance there's a *Darlin' Corey graveyard* lonesomeness to it.

The Huff girls taught me to carry the mourning doves' sound with me, to make an oval jar-shape with my two hands and blow in the hole between my thumbs. By blowing harder and softer I can get all three of the notes to come out.

But in later years, only the cry of the throaty dove itself will conjure up this scene again.

MRS. SIMMS

In our landlady's house, I remember so well the variety of crocheted doilies spread on every dark table, me lolling on the plush davenport, enjoying funny moving patterns in the gently shifting chiffon curtains.

Politeness gripped my mother to the overstuffed chair with the antimacassar as our hostess lit one cigarette off of another, telling her oft-told tale, always with new details, of losing her twins, her abdominal surgery, and her hemorrhoids.

I was amazed at how the cigarette would stick to her lower lip as she talked, curls of smoke unfurling playfully as my poor mother suppressed yawn after yawn.

BIBLE LESSONS

They had one of us read a verse in the Bible after the salute to the flag every morning at school. (Perfunctory, yes, but even if your parents didn't attend to your Bible education, you couldn't say you'd never heard it).

A two-week Bible school at the Baptist church across the playground, across the creek, across Orchard Creek Road, was held while school was in session. We got extended recesses to attend. Everyone did.

A lady in the basement room told us the streets in heaven were paved with gold. I said, "They'd be too heavy, they'd fall down."

"If it's in the Bible, its true. The Lord's Word."

And she gave us plaster of Paris to pour in "God is Love" molds.

Upstairs in the sanctuary, I held the beautiful watered-silk cover of the hymnal and moved it around in the light while the preacher's voice rolled over us. He asked for a volunteer.

Buddy came up. "Now, this thread is like a sin," he said, binding Buddy's wrist with one strand. Now, break it! It popped, and Buddy smirked. But you keep sinning…the preacher said, wrapping the thread again and again. "Now break it." Buddy struggled. That got my attention. "We're born sinners … Look deep into yourself …" And I learned to look deep at a tender age. (Do we even try anymore? As stupid as I thought the hacknyed, overwrought evangelical patter was, it made us try.)

Finally, the choir director had us sing, "Ope, Ope the Gates of Day." It sounded so weird, it was hard for any of us to sing without snickering.

BIBLE SCHOOL

The sweetness of sorrow
I felt often when young.
to read of distress
enobled my own.

They taught us at church
that suffering had worth.
At thirteen I could feel it
and measure my growth.

EASTER

With dedication and fasting we gathered
to feel the Resurrection.
We came in darkness
to feel the energy that surges
in bird calls and whispering grasses
moments before the sun appears.

Impossible to embrace
what we might have found
that morning
marred by the desecration
from the pastor who broke
the golden silence
with staccato words
without mercy or joy.

ODE TO SENATOR TALMADGE

Some voices imply rooms of another era, their timbre soft as cedar shavings underfoot, penetrating wherever they happen to be like oil on the wood floor, approaching us down the lengthy corridor with an amber tone of oak desks and chairs of yellow window shades, of flypaper hung in high-ceilinged rooms, littered with pieties.

HEADING NORTH

Hardy songbirds came through last week
descendants of old acquaintances
with an unexpected shipment:
never used memories
—murmuring meadows
the bright edges of petals
from an apple blossom
an abandoned chimney
located inland, far to the South
of long ago.

SPELUNKERS

From time out of mind spelunkers lived here.
Their valley was green and pancake-flat,
limestone ridges between quartzite.
Where they went down was an open secret.

What held a claim on their minds was
an underground river which in its many branchings
underlay all, connecting all.
Deep dropoffs and its meanderings confounded
efforts to grasp its extent.
The valley's topside blessings were hazy mornings,
sycamore's white silhouettes against the dark ridges,
its dependable fertility.
But to grow more than one needed, to argue
over boundaries seemed small-minded.
Business-oriented outlanders who settled there
dismissed the underlying geology.
Their interest was acreage.
They had intended to buy up every farm, one by one
but found they were blocked for the most part
by the natives in their iron-clad loyalty to the land.
Every so often a corner of pasture would cave in.
Most outlanders regarded the sink holes as monstrous
nuisances, sepulcres for cows.
A few would find themselves seesawing between
curiosity and alarm at the treacherousness of the earth.
When they overcame their fear, the cave-ins
were their excuse to shed the distain and
go down to share the absorbing preoccupation
of the gentle, reckless natives.

BALDS AND COVES

In the summer in the Smokies, even the second or third-growth was so thick, you couldn't see out. And deep in the park was some real primeval forest. Near Alum Rock Cave, the wild rhodadendron and laurel were so sturdy that mountaineers with big shoes bragged that you could walk across on the top of them, "if'n you knowed how." In one valley grove, the naturalist measured an old tulip maple with a 34-foot circumferance.

The destination of most hikes was a fire lookout tower, where you could get above it all and see a few identifiable peaks, ridge after ridge of furrowed landscape, in a progression from green to pale blue.

The bear went over the mountain, the bear went over the mountain. The bear went over the mountain, and what do you think he saw? He saw another mountain... It seemed endless, though you knew from experience that seven miles from Gatlinburg, in Pigeon Forge (birthplace of Dolly Parton), it flattened out.

"When'll we be there?" we'd pester Mr. Stupka, the naturalist. "Oh, about lunchtime."

We trudged on, on muddy paths, fording a creek here and there in a patch of sun, stopping to watch a millepede move its legs in wavey motion. We ate lunch at 1:30 pm.

I loved going into the fire towers, and talking to the fire lookout men. But more than once I got stymied coming down. I never was any good at country bridges where you could see the water below between the planks, or even at hopping rocks in the creek, so this was no surprise. I sat on my butt, and they coaxed me down while I did the stairs sitting down.

Of course, the view was fabulous from the two tallest peaks, Clingmans Dome and Mt. Leconte. Clingmans Dome was close to the highway, a short hike through Canadian flora of Balsam and moss. Some of these plants had been wiped out in New England and Europe during the Ice Age. A visiting woman geologist from Switzerland walking here enthused, "Oh, I feel just like I'm right back in the Eocene!"

Mt. LeConte was seven miles off the road. The family was glad when I was big enough to walk it. We came in by the beautiful deep forest path where the sturdy rhodadendrons grew, and straggled into the lodge on top at dusk. We were greeted by the uncle of my classmates in the Huff family. Our host looked just like Gary Cooper.

To bed in rough wooden cabins with Hudson's Bay blankets, roused out of bed, sore, early to watch the sunrise over the dusky blue panorama, mist rising between numerous ridges (giving the Smokies their name). Wood smoke meant breakfast. After enormous pancakes and some bacon, (they packed supplies in by mule), we left by another trail, over a sunnier route. The face we were descending had accordian pleats of ridges. Each fold had two kinds of trees, according to the exposure. I loved best the pine trees on the west sides in the warm afternoon sun.

This got us down to Cherokee Orchard, where a friend met us. This is as close as we ever got to camping out, because Philip, after hiking and doing geology all day, wanted to be in-side!

Other destinations were balds and coves.

Balds were mountaintops where no trees grew, owing to curious soil conditions. The toughest trip was Andrew's Bald, but worth it in spring for the fields of wild azaleas in bloom. I think Philip had a list of hikes like scoutmasters have lists of badges to be earned. So, at last I graduated to the level of making this hike. It was a miserable grey day, and my most vivid memory is of a humongous rattler that someone killed.

Coves were easy: you could drive in. They were wide, flat valleys of limestone between the ridges. They had always been cultivated, and even in the park the government made a point of letting the old-timers stay in Wades Cove, to show the rest of us how it was in log-cabin times.

In most instances, the mountaineers were moved off the land when it became a park in 1943. Old topo maps my father used showed buildings, but if he lit out toward one in a storm, he was likely to find it in a field of wet saplings, abandoned and caving in. I interviewed a woman for a high school essay who had been moved. The family had done extremely well with their tourist court in Gatlinburg, but she practically wept as she thought of the beauty of the place they had left.

Off at the edges of these limestone valleys there were sinkholes, and in rare instances, caves.

SCOURED EARTH

Toads and roosters spoke to us
through the hum of bugs and moos and baahs.
White oak leaves had the smell of tea
and sweet whiffs of distant manure.
Gone, all washed away, except in memory.
How perfectly we level our suburban meadows!

DRIVING THERE

There's a concrete-belted abstraction between me and the land.
From a smooth divided highway all the hills look bland.

I'm not asking for the old road that made outlanders cringe.
(It tried to save on farmland by winding along the ridge.)

Preserve the alternate routes so the hills don't slide by so quick.
I want to see what trees they have images of them will stick.

I want to smell wood smoke when I roll the window down,
I want to hear the katydids before I get to town.

ROOSTER

The crowing
of the rooster
at the nearby school
where there's a "farm"
takes me right back to Tennessee
at our home beside Max Watson's farm
fifty years ago.

Fifty years on,
one of the kids at this school
will be helping
in a small village in the outskirts of nowhere.
Some goofy rooster will awaken her
in the dead of night
por la madrugada,
blown right back
to her days
at a school in subrubia.

TRUDGING

Oh, Lordie, it's so hot I caint go on.
All these weeds and saplings crowding the trail!
Never mind your bug bites, child,
Gotta keep an eye out for snakes!
Keep your sleeves rolled down, there's poison ivy!

Smells mix in my nose
cowshit with honeysuckle
dust with tobacco plants

I plod on.

Sounds mix in my ears
the buzz of bees
the come and go, whine of *skeeters*
sudden zips of grasshoppers
and through all the sizzle of katydids,
who've known since dawn:
It's a Hot One!

Chickens everywhere.

Gotta go back, it's cloudin' over.
Feel the wind?
Come on, let's git back
before the big ol' raindrops gitcha.

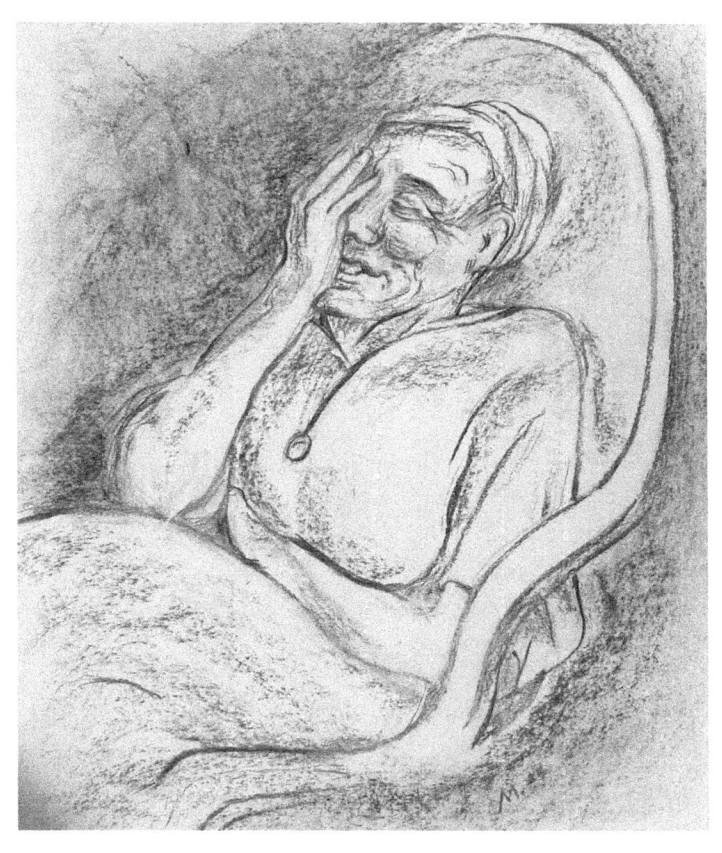

V.

WESTTOWN FRIENDS SCHOOL, 1951-1954

I was sent to a Quaker boarding school near Philadelphia
—a caring, intellectual environment
where social justice and mysticism were discussed.

*When I was young
I could already feel the
sustained sadness of trees.
Their leaves moved on high
in large processions, gravely.
At these I gazed each day
stealing glimpses while in class.*

WHEN I WAS YOUNG

When
I was young
I could already feel the
sustained sadness of trees.
Their leaves moved on high
in large processions, gravely.
At these I gazed each day
stealing glimpses while in class.
Towering branches appeared
as leaves fell away
throughout
the autumn.
In their
spirit
I saw
my
own,
mute
but
majestic.

PREMONITION

Even before I had
a lover to love
I heard the wet
rustle of leaves
in the trees above.

I sought after
plants I fancied
scented with musk
I enthralled myself
among stately trees
in the dusk.

AUTOMAT OF THE INTELLECT

Dusty radiators fume and bake the air
sporadically sewage moves inside the wall
of the two-century-old dormitory.
Cosmetic odors of former students
hover and diffuse
forced from the wall by a hot light bulb.

The sound of doors to other rooms, footfalls, ticking clocks
all become matters of indifference.
My eyes make their appointed rounds through Proust.

Beyond the rooms with translucent sweaty windows
the Connecticut River rapids roils up cold shrapnel
welts in the darkness.
My eyes hesitate.

A dim oceanic rumble of traffic fills the pause.

For a moment the mind is remote, out in the wind.
In the slate-gray evening
seeing the damp trees' silhouette against
a high wall of yellow windows.

Each like a food-filled aperture in the Automat,
a well-lit vignette behind glass
inviting me to partake.

HOAGIES

"You've never had a hoagie?" I hadn't been at the school as a freshman like my companion, so I was in the dark. "Well, come on!"

We were in West Chester for two hours for once-a-month shopping. It was about four miles from Westtown, and we had been brought by our school's bus, or a strange hand-built stretch limosine we called the Lizard cobbled together out of several Chryslers painted an ugly green.

In a mad rush to buy stationery supplies that the school store didn't carry, underwear, cute blouses, new nylon hose, we found our way to a deli where my classmate got a Hoagie for each of us.

Back at the dorm, the whole floor smelled of Hoagie before we even unwrapped ours, oozing out of the rooms of fifteen other classmates.

I ate mine and my throat and eyes burned. I couldnt finish the thing right away. I wasn't sure I was happy I had tried it or not (the way I felt about my first cigarette).

This was my introduction to raw garlic and hot peppers. that came with olive oil and lots of Italian meats—salami and others—with two or three aromatic cheeses placed in a Italian bread roll.

Why Hoagies? Why Philly?

When I became accustomed to the smell and taste, I loved it. It became an addiction I addressed once a month when I went into town.

With our weekend workcamp group that took place in downtown Philadelphia, we wandered out of the Black neighborhood into: Little Italy where Italians were bargaining in sidewalk markets and delicatessens that sold Hoagies.

This is the neighborhood where many popular Italian American singers hailed from—Mario Lanza, Al Martino, and Frankie Avalon. Hearing their voices later, I thought of and yearned for a Hoagie. Upon my return to the area for a class reunion, I sought out and enjoyed one that brought me back to Philly, my own version of Proust's Madelaine.

WONDER DRUG

Penicillin, invented just in time
to save GIs fighting against Hitler,
and also my mother in 1947.

We shopped in the town where
they made it, West Chester, PA.
The factory chimneys burped
a hot banana-and-vinegar odor.

From the Acme Market
to the A & P, we endured
the fumes with extra good grace
for the sake of humanity.

VISIT HOME

Any dumb job would free mother
from choking and holding her tongue

Make divorce an unspoken possibility

And free me from her sorrow told in mime

HARKENING BACK

At the National Gallery
in an alcove
I found a small painting
of Parisian walls
whose milky grays
drab ochres and russets bricks
so exactly matched
the walls of my perpetually
overcast Philadephia adolesence
that tears sprang out of me.

And in Vienna
I found a room full of
Bruegels with my favorite
Hunters in the Snow among them
returning at twilight
writ larger than I ever imagined
and darker, too:
It is nightfall and cold.
The hunters with their many dogs
trudge down the steep slope
to the village where a small square
that never shows in reproductions
glows orange. It's the distant
window of a hut.
I'm shivering with the snow
that covers the hunters' boots.
Taken aback by the far-off
promise of a warm hearth,
I cry.

On my own turf
under cloudless western skies
I stand before a scene in
a Charles Burchfield painting
a truly ugly brick factory
adjacent to a black iron
railroad trestle
a murky river flowing
under it through
soot-stained snow.

My chest grew tight
feeling again
all those harsh winters
in Philadephia
with a hate that inspires
a grim affection.

"It reminds me of the East,"
I told my companion
all choked up.

DIMENSIONS

I

We pause on the wooded slope
our toes pointed downward
enveloped by the fully fleshed-out leaves
of late spring. A small green room.

High above, unseen
a prolonged warble.
A distant answering
trill
and our chamber
becomes transpaent.

II

Not all day, for it's too cold
trudging for several hours in the afternoon
we trudge with numb legs
in the snow
making new tracks
on a vacant landscape
till white and gray turn to slate blue.
No telling where we're at!

A breath of smoke:
                Humankind!

PORTRAITS OF SELF-AWARENESS

YOUTH
BEWILDERED

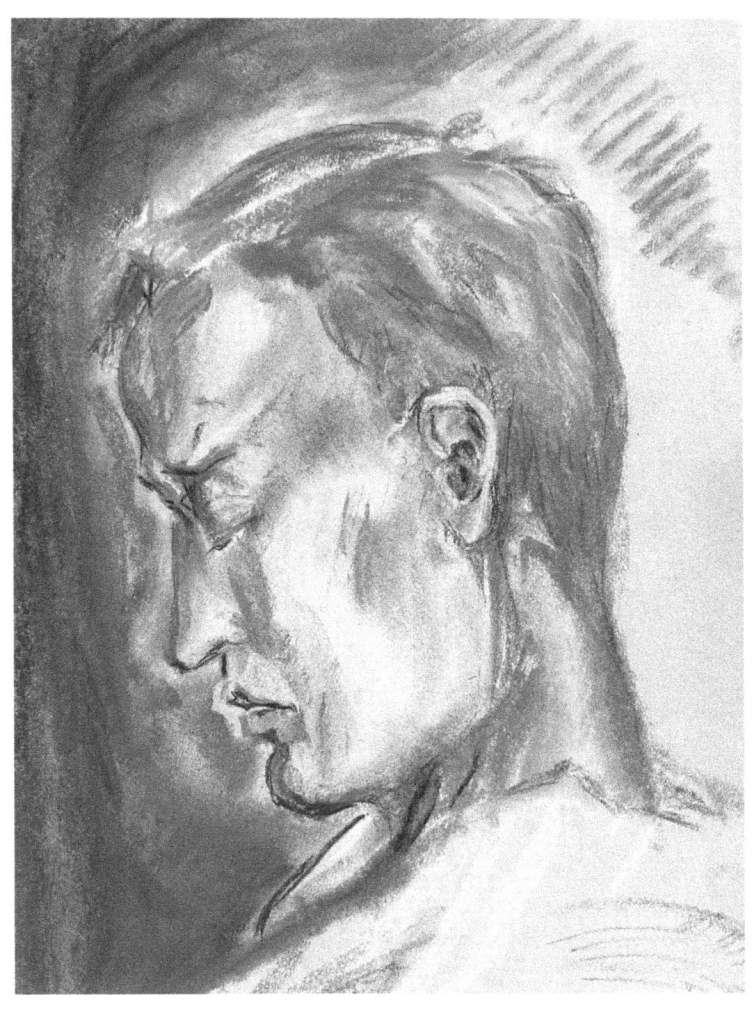

YOUTH OF
FERVENT DEDICATION

WOMAN OF
COMPOSURE

WOMAN OF
WISDOM & COMPASSION

LIST OF ILLUSTRATIONS

✸ ✸ ✸

Page 2 – Photo of Helen and Philip King by Myrrh in 1954.

Page 4 – *So like my mother!* photo. (Source unknown)

In both her pose in profile and early 1920s aesthetic, the woman here has an uncanny resemblance to my mother.

Page 8 – Pennsylvania Autumn. Watercolor by the author at age 16.

Autumn leaves of native trees on the West Coast don't turn red like those on the East Coast.

Page 10 – Winter Orchard. Watercolor by the author at age 16.

Page 18 – Georgetown Mansion, Dutch Elm Trees.

These graceful trees died in a blight; other species have taken their place.

Page 26 and 35 – Hotel Windows. Pencil drawing by the author.

The losses of patriarchal families in the South made itself felt to me in their attention to Civil War etiquette like teaching me to curtesy. It made families eligible for social climbing. Their frowns and coaching did me no good.

Page 38 – Reagan Furniture Shop. Pen and ink drawing for Westtown assignment, "Home Town Essay" by the author at age 16.

Gatlinburg was full of Reagans since colonial days. I learned that my husband Daryl Reagan had relatives in Tennessee. An aunt of his interested in joining the Daughters of the American Revolution traced the family back to the very county where Gatlinburg is located. They arrived about 1650, and they likely had traces of Elizabethan dialect in their mountaineer speech.

Page 43 – Grist Mill, Pigeon Forge. Watercolor by the author at age 17.

Hometown of Dolly Parton. Tourist accommodations have replaced the meadows that I loved, but the old grist mill remains. Rotating stones, powered by water power, ground the farmers' corn for making cornbread.

Page 44 – Mt. LeConte, oblique view. Pen and ink drawing by Myrrh's father, Philip B. King.

Geology of the area proved to be a great puzzle. It took six geologists eight years to unravel it. King illustrated his professional papers with these remarkable drawings.

Page 51 – Abandoned Mountain Cabin. Watercolor by the author at age 12.

Mountaineers moving away to make room for the Great Smoky Mountains National Park left some abandoned buildings behind. With lush rainfall, saplings quickly grew in the open fields around them. People who were moved off were often very homesick for living in the woods.

Page 52 – Leaf-burning Smoke. Watercolor by the author at age 12.

Along with the misty smoke, the incense-like smell of burning leaves was enchanting.

Page 57 – Hillside Tobacco Farm. Watercolor by the author at age 13.

Note the two figures on the road below. To go into a barn where they were drying tobacco was a sensory experience! It smells very good when not being smoked.

Page 60 – House in Dudley Creek Hollow. Watercolor by the author at age 12.

The windowsills were painted sky blue with geranium window boxes. This notch in the hills was so well hidden from our house in Gatlinburg that I didn't discover it until I lived there for two years.

Page 65 – Latrine with Birdhouses Made of Gourds. Pen and ink for Westtown assignment, "Home Town Essay" by the author at age 16.

About half the students came from far away, which made this assignment fitting.

Page 69 – The Pleasure of Remembering. Charcoal drawing by the author at age 87.

While contemplating this book, the image of this woman came to me in a reverie.

Page 70 – Westtown School. Watercolor by the author age 17.

During my senior year in high school, my class schedule had two study hall periods together. The art teacher gave me permission to draw outdoors.

Page 74 – Westtown Woods. Pastel by the author at age 17.

Page 83 – Leaf. Pen and ink drawing by the author.

A study in patterns that branch at varying scales.

Pages 84-87 – Portraits of Self-Awareness. Pastels by the author at ages between 15 and 17.

Page 84 – Youth Bewildered.

Shows my feelings of lostness at the new school. When my teacher Marty Gleisser from Switzerland saw this, she immediately showed me her precious etchings by Kathe Kollwitz. This gave me confidence to become a woman artist.

Page 85 – Youth of Fervent Dedication.

I went three times a year to do Quaker service work in the Philadelphia slums, and that ignited a fire inside me for social activism.

Page 86 – Woman of Composure.

I saw her as an archetypal figure who was maturing as an individual and developing high ideals.

Page 87 – Woman of Wisdom and Compassion.

An archetypal figure that is an homage to the older Quaker women in my life.

ACKNOWLEDGEMENTS

✶ ✶ ✶

Marty Giessler—Teacher from Switzerland, who was so touched at the drawing Bewildered, 1951, done when I was 15, that she showed me her treasured etchings by Kathe Kollwitz. I never doubted from that moment on women could make great art.

David Richie—Leader of the Weekend Workcamp project Philadelphia, one where we were invited into homes to help them cover their coal-black rooms with pastel paint. I attended a total of 10 times in three years, and took part in his discussions of "why there are slums."

Daryl Reagan—My husband, a physicist who admitted that he didn't understand art, but was proud of what I was doing and provided the support for me to do my art.

Theodor Jung—Photographer, calligrapher, and book designer, my only male mentor from 1973 until 1980. The absence of support of women artists by most men provoked women to assert themselves and realize their potential.

Edith Smith—Professor at Foothill College, who mentored me in particular for 30 years from 1967-1990. She started an artist support group that continued even after her death. This encouraged us even when we sold nothing.

Ruth Waters—Sculptor and founder of an art museum plus artist studios—three times! She urged me to be professional. I had a studio in her first effort at Twin Pines Art Center in 1977.

Robert Perry—Book designer and editor of this book and my *Essential Mysteries in Art and Science*. Founder of Robert Perry Book Design and Dutch Poet Press in Palo Alto, California.

Sylvia Martin, my Girl Friday, for her dedication, thoughtfulness, and invaluable assistance and support. I cannot do all that do without her.

COLOPHON

Cover and interior design done by Robert Perry
Robert Perry Book Design and Dutch Poet Press
Palo Alto, California.

Printed and distributed by IngramSpark.

Display and body text set in Centaur
designed by Bruce Rogers and Frederic Warde
in 1914 and released in 1929.

www.ingramcontent.com/pod-product-compliance
Lightning Source LLC
Chambersburg PA
CBHW061739070526
44585CB00024B/2737